SCOTLAND

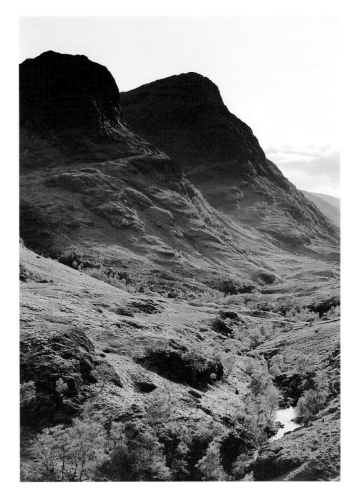

This edition produced for Barnes & Noble Books in 2002 by
Colin Baxter Photography Ltd.
Grantown-on-Spey, PH26 3NA, Scotland

A CIP catalogue record for this book is available from the British Library

ISBN 0-7607-3647-2

Printed in China

Front Cover Photograph: Beinn Sgulaird and Loch Creran, Argyll
Page 1 Photograph: 'The Three Sisters', Glencoe
Page 3 Photograph: The Red Cuillin across Broadford Bay, Isle of Skye
Back Cover Photograph: Loch Maddy, North Uist

SCOTLAND

COLIN BAXTER

BARNES
& NOBLE
BOOKS
NEW YORK

SCOTLAND

The image of Scotland portrayed in many places is a confused and often inaccurate one. The clear blue skies and ever-green grass throughout endless brochures and many publications mix uneasily with exaggerated preconceptions of wall-to-wall tartan, wee stone cottages, midges galore, the cold, and perpetual rain.

There are all these things, but most of the time there is a more realistic side to a country that is visually rich, atmospheric and diverse. The photographs here show just a part of this world.

The Scottish landscape varies enormously from north to south, east to west and Highland to Lowland, with these differences magnified by the seasonal changes to colour, light and weather. Indeed, if it wasn't for Scotland's changeable weather, most of the places shown on these pages would look very different, and being there would feel very different too.

For a small country, there are some disadvantages in sitting directly in the line of fire for depressions spinning across the Atlantic Ocean. But there are advantages too, and not just for photographers.

Glencoe in the summer with the sky clear is impressive, though the mountains can look almost like cardboard cutouts. But to drive through the glen in the wake of an autumn storm is another experience altogether — early snow on the tops, vivid oranges and browns lit by streaming beams of sunlight through dramatic clouds still racing southwards.

You must stop, it will be gone in minutes, even seconds, that special moment — the weather, the light and the land combining magically to produce an invigorating and completely different feeling to that of a still summer day.

It is that very feeling, the sense of what it is like, being there, that I am trying to capture with the camera. Grabbing rectangles,

I often call it. Scotland offers a myriad of wonderful settings within its landscape and throughout the seasons. However, it is very much 'off season' that the land is at its most exciting. The fresh greens of spring, the golds of autumn and through into winter when a subtle array of blues, purples, greys and whites adds to the palette. But it is the nature of the light through those long winter months that really produces the atmosphere — warm and oblique all day, sculpting the hills and glens back to their real, very three-dimensional shapes.

One final element often completes the picture — snow. Without it the mountains aren't quite the same and when a covering reaches down to sea level, the landscape takes on a less familiar but very beautiful guise. Look at the photograph opposite; Eilean Donan Castle on a fairly rare day. I felt privileged sitting there as the sun and clouds staged a spectacle of light over the vista, before the curtain of dusk came down on that brief afternoon.

Scotland has also had a long and eventful history, the physical remnants of which, from the revered to the humble, add yet another dimension to the country and its landscape. Castles, brochs, standing stones, and the remains of simple homes scatter the land. Combined with the light they too can instil a special feeling of again just being there.

So here is a personal selection of places and moments gleaned from many years exploring throughout the country. Scotland may be small but its landscape is a rich tapestry that harbours a wealth of impressive situations to experience, savour and enjoy.

Colin Baxter

Eilean Donan Castle and Loch Alsh (*opposite*)

Ben Lomond and Loch Ard, Trossachs *(opposite)*
Stones of Stenness, Orkney *(above)*

Iona and the Sound of Iona from Erraid, Isle of Mull

Lossit Bay, Islay

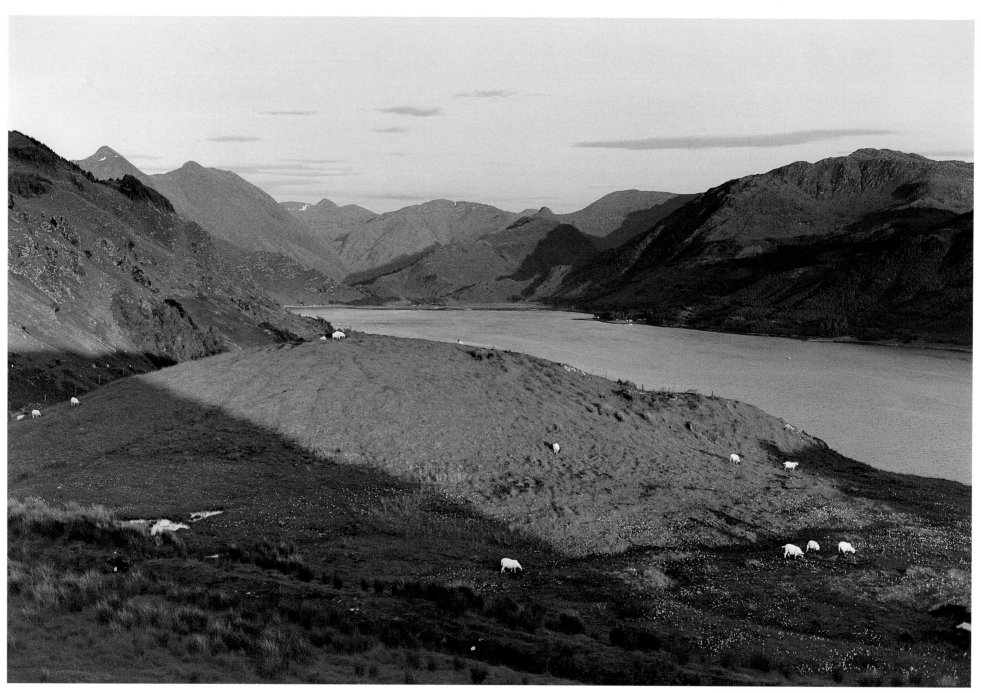

Loch Duich and the Kintail Mountains

Loch Awe, Argyll

II

Loch an Eilein, Rothiemurchus, Cairngorms

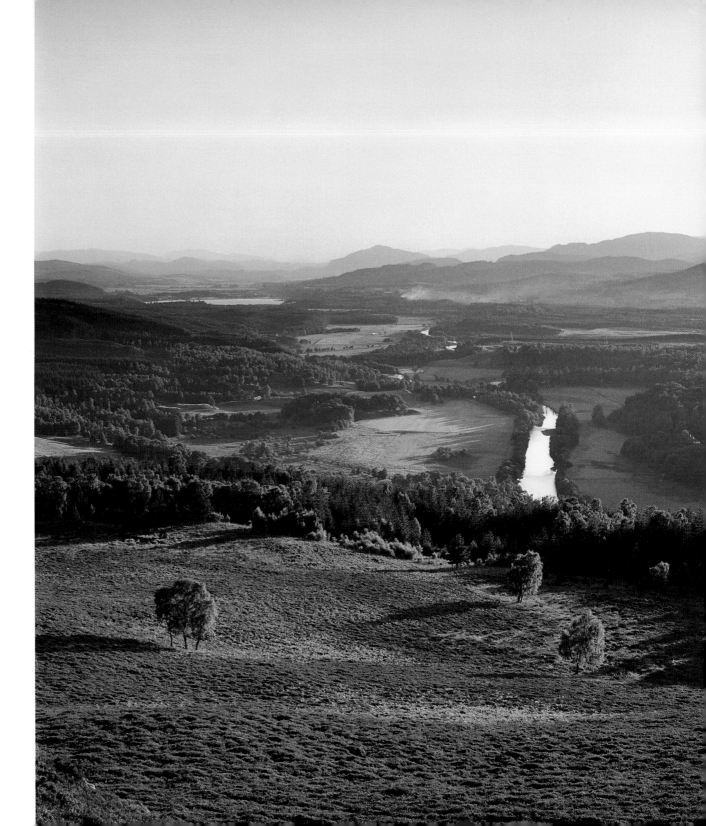

Loch Insh and the River Spey, Strathspey

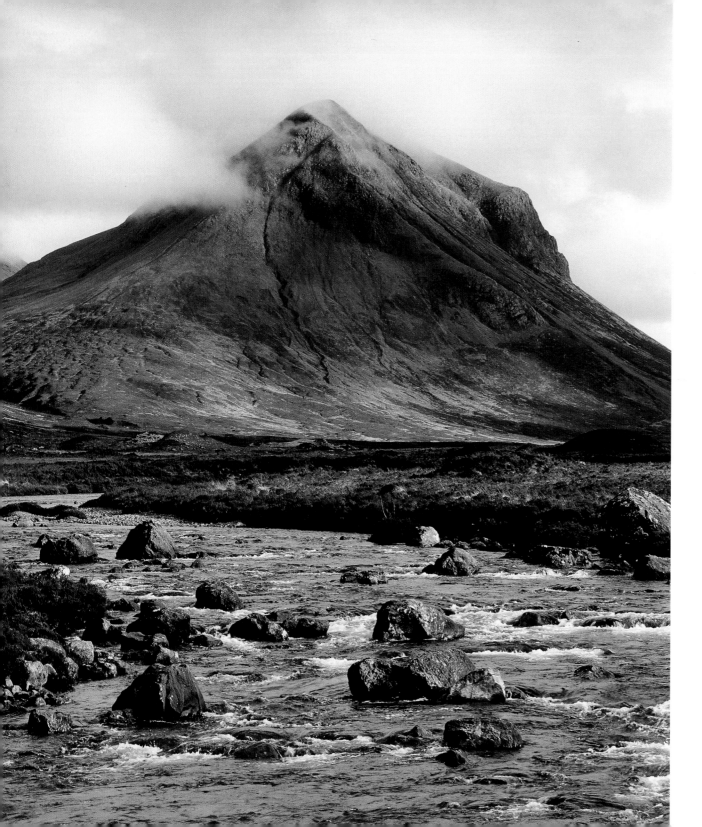

Marsco and the River Sligachan, Isle of Skye

The River Earn, Strathearn and the Ochil Hills, Perthshire

Beinn Damh and Loch Damh across Loch Torridon, Wester Ross

Eshaness, Northmavine, Shetland

The River Spey at Boat of Garten (*above*)
The Five Sisters of Kintail, Shiel Bridge and Loch Duich (*opposite*)

Ben Cruachan and Loch Etive, Argyll *(opposite)*
Suilven, Sutherland *(above)*

Spynie Palace, Moray

Loch Morar, The Sound of Sleat and Island of Eigg

Ben Venue and Loch Katrine, Trossachs

Ben Cruachan, Argyll

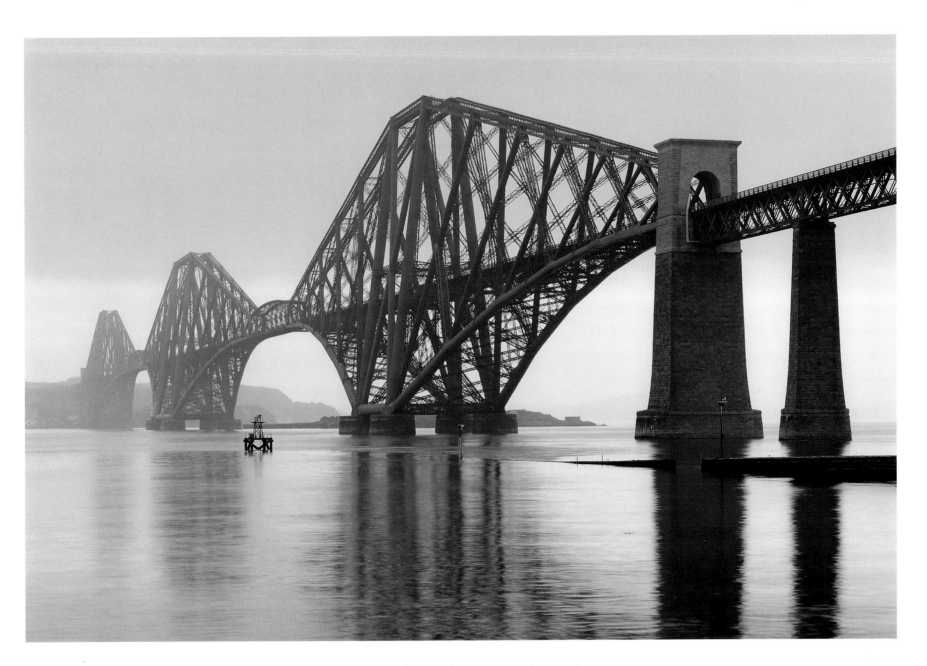

Edinburgh Castle and city *(opposite)*
The Forth Bridge *(above)*

27

Handa Island and Point of Stoer, Sutherland

Ettrick, Borders

Stob Coire Easain, Glen Spean and Loch Laggan, Badenoch

Ben More, Isle of Mull

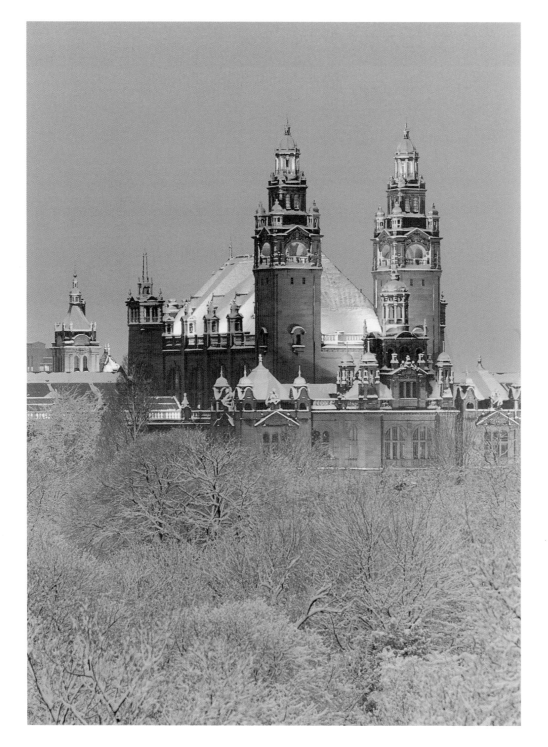

Kelvingrove Art Gallery
and Museum, Glasgow *(left)*
The Cuillin Hills, Isle of Skye *(opposite)*

Kyles of Bute, Argyll *(opposite)*
Bàgh an Tigh-Stòir, Craignish, Argyll *(above)*

35

Tràigh Scarasta and Chaipaval, Harris

Ardtalnaig and Loch Tay, Perthshire

Loch Achray, Trossachs

Ben Nevis and Loch Eil

Ardvreck Castle and Loch Assynt, Sutherland *(above)*
Ben Challum and Glen Lochay, Breadalbane *(opposite)*

The Cairngorms and Upper Deeside *(opposite)*
Eigg from Arisaig, Lochaber *(above)*

Loch Muick, Aberdeenshire

Braes of Glenlivet, Moray

Loch Gruinart, Islay

Eilean na h-Aiteig, Oldshore Beg, Sutherland

Carrbridge, Strathspey

Cawdor Castle, Nairnshire

Balephuil Bay, Tiree

Cairn Toul, Cairngorms

Dunnottar Castle, Aberdeenshire

The Lairig Ghru, Cairngorms

Glen Affric

Blair Castle, Perthshire

Mingulay from Berneray, Outer Hebrides

Near Elsrickle, South Lanarkshire

Tràigh Bàn nam Manach, Iona

Iona Abbey

Sands of Forvie and the River Ythan, Aberdeenshire

Abernethy Forest and Meall a' Bhuachaille, Strathspey

Stac Pollaidh, Wester Ross *(above)*
Loch Ness and Urquhart Castle *(opposite)*

Loch Laggan, Badenoch *(opposite)*
Braeriach, Cairngorms *(above)*

The Ross of Mull and Ardmeanach, Isle of Mull *(above)*
Lake of Menteith, Stirlingshire *(opposite)*

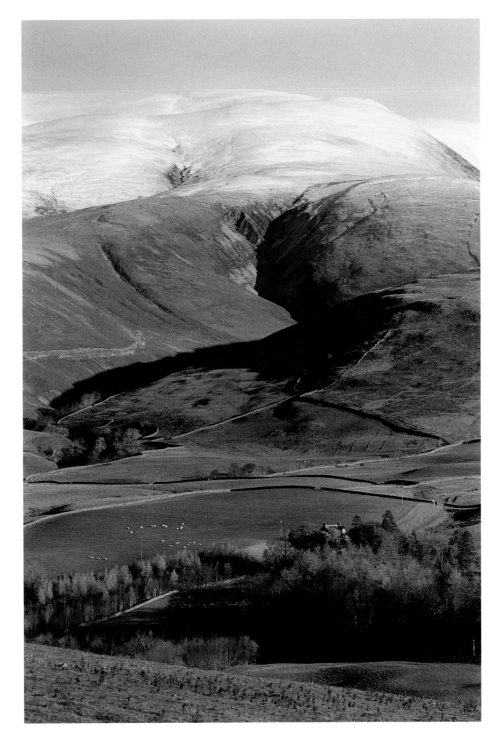

Coire an t-Sneachda, Cairngorms *(opposite)*
Hart Fell and Upper Annandale, Borders *(right)*

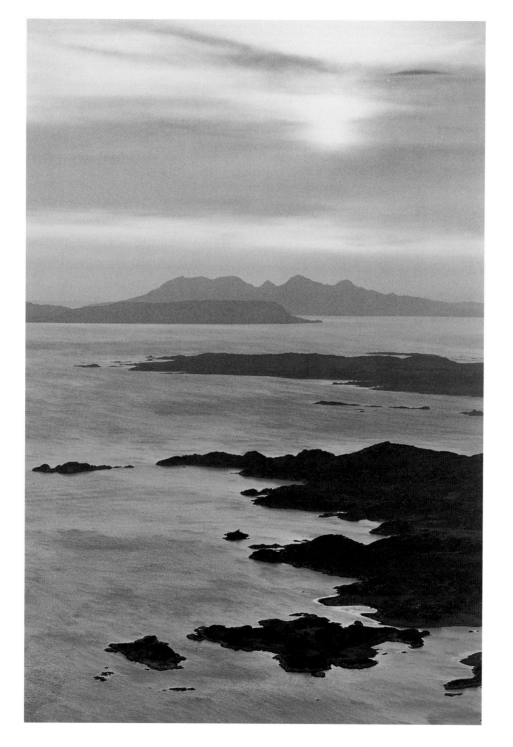

Rum, Eigg and the Sound of Arisaig

Boreray and Stacs from across Loch a' Ghlinne, Hirta, St Kilda

Pass of Killiecrankie, Perthshire

The Eildon Hills, Borders

Gruinard Bay, Wester Ross

Inverpolly across Achnahaird Bay, Wester Ross

Balmoral Castle, Deeside *(above)*
The River Dee, Lochnagar and Balmoral Castle *(opposite)*

Glenfinnan Monument and Loch Shiel, Lochaber *(opposite)*
Beinn Resipol and Loch Sunart, by Ardnamurchan *(above)*

Corran Seilebost, Harris

Gigha Island, Sound of Gigha and Kintyre, Argyll

Lochan na h-Earba, Badenoch

Loch Pityoulish, Strathspey

Glen Clunie, Aberdeenshire

Lochnagar across Glen Callater, Aberdeenshire

Calanais Standing Stones, Lewis *(left)*
The North Harris Hills and Tràigh Rosamol,
Luskentyre, Harris *(opposite)*

Liath Bheinn, Ben Avon and the River Avon, Moray *(opposite)*
Towards Lochnagar from the Lecht, Aberdeenshire *(above)*

Derry Cairngorm and Loch Etchachan across Loch Avon, Cairngorms

Bidean nam Bian, Glencoe

Loch Laidon, Rannoch Moor

Stob a' Choin and Loch Katrine, Strath Gartney, Trossachs

Dunnet Bay, Caithness *(above)*
The Cuillin Ridge, Loch Coruisk and Loch Scavaig, Isle of Skye *(opposite)*

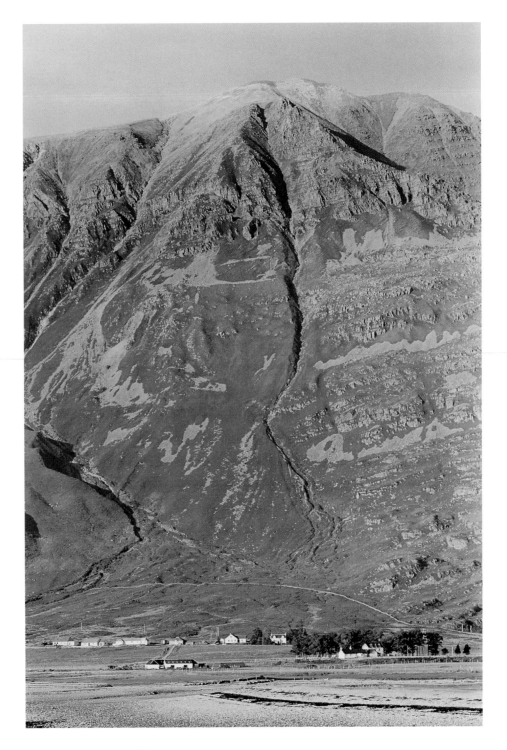

Castle Stalker, Appin, Argyll *(opposite)*
Liathach, Torridon, Wester Ross *(right)*

The River Avon at Achlichnie,
Strath Avon, Moray

Glen Brown, Braes of Abernethy and the Cairngorms

Corgarff Castle, Upper Donside, Aberdeenshire

The Village, Hirta, St Kilda

Loch Ness, looking south-west *(above)*
Loch Lomond, with the islands of Inchcailloch and Clairinsh in the foreground *(opposite)*

102

The Storr and Old Man of Storr across Loch Fada, Trotternish, Isle of Skye *(opposite)*
Cùl Beag and Stac Pollaidh, Inverpolly, Wester Ross *(above)*

Isle of Jura from above Tayvallich, Argyll

Loch Affric, Glen Affric

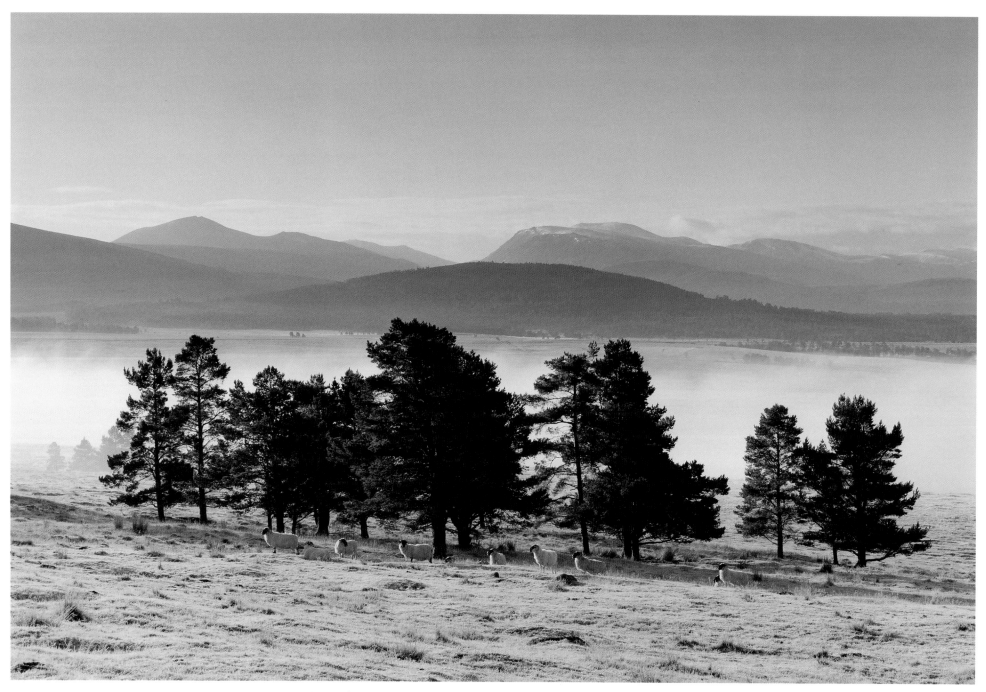

Bynack More and Cairn Gorm across Abernethy Forest

Glen Lyon, Perthshire

Loch Fyne at Ardno, Argyll *(above)*
The Cuillin Hills, Bla Bheinn and Loch Dùghaill, Sleat, Isle of Skye *(opposite)*

INDEX OF PLACES